HAVE YOU EVER LOVED A COW?

By Alexis Short
Illustrated by Wendy Jacobs

COPYRIGHT @ 2024 WENDY JACOBS - ARTWORK
ISBN 979-8-218-36508-0

For Bret, Mav, Foxy, and Rookie

You are never too old to set another goal
or to dream another dream.
-C.S. Lewis

"Have you ever loved a cow?" my Grandma said to me.

"A cow can be a good best friend.
Come to the farm and see!"

Grandma grabbed her milk can
and we walked on down the lane,

She held my hand and laughed with me,
calling to the pigs by name.

And when we made it to the fence
we opened up the gate,

We weren't at all surprised to see Molly munching on some hay.

Grandma fills the milk can
singing as she goes,

And when she's done she won't forget to pat Molly on her nose.

"Cows really are so special," she says
"They give us yummy treats!"

"Yogurt, ice cream, chocolate bars, and LOTS of milk to drink!"

We start our walk back to the house
the sunshine starts to fade,

Milk can in hand, Grandma smiles and says,
"Have you ever loved a cow?"

The End

A note from the author-

Hi! My name is Lexi. I enjoy spending time with my boys, running, taking pictures, and baking. When I became a mother, I lost myself a little bit. Every now and then, bits and pieces of who I am find their way to the surface. This project was one of those pieces. I didn't know I wanted to publish a children's book. The idea totally shook me. But here we are! My Grandma Yoyo inspired this book, and Wendy brought it to life with her artwork. I encourage you to do the things that seem impossible. I believe that it is in those moments we find great purpose and joy!

Made in the USA
Las Vegas, NV
07 February 2024